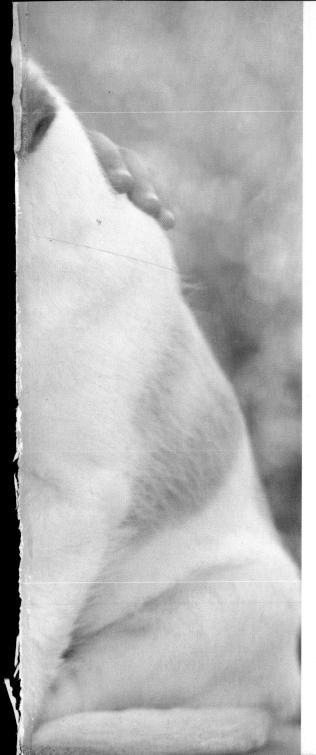

Gerd Ludwig

Sit! Stay!

Train Your Dog the Easy Way

Photography: Monika Wegler

Drawings: Renate Holzner

Translated from the German by Eric A. Bye

D1473562

BARI

CONTENTS

THE WAY DOGS ARE

- Social creatures

- Need a secure place in the family "pack"

- Need contact in play and competitive sport with other dogs

- Accept a human as leader of the pack

- Want to have a job to do

- Are capable of learning and adjusting

- Love regular activity

- Come in more than 400 distinct breeds

Dogs have been faithful companions to humans for almost 15,000 years. They inherited from their wolf ancestors a readiness to fit into society and to acknowledge the leader of the pack. Thanks to their extraordinary ability to learn, dogs adapt to very diverse living conditions and have become dependable partners in all leisure-time activities. They are alert companions, guardians and defenders, patient listeners, and soul soothers. They gladly help their owners with their work: herding, hunting, rescuing, and protecting their homes from two-legged and four-legged intruders. But for all that, they cling to their wolf heritage and their characteristic needs. Dogs are fleet-footed beasts of prey. They need games to take the place of hunting, keep them physically fit, challenge their mind, and satisfy their natural instincts. Dogs need the closeness of their human pack and the guiding hand of their master; they need affection and contact with other dogs.

UNDERSTANDING DOG BEHAVIOR

Dogs are social creatures. Their ability to learn makes it easy for them to fit into the partnership with humans. The basis for effective communication is an understanding of their fundamental behavior.

What Dogs Need

Three things are essential to the happiness of a family dog: an intact human/dog pack, a human pack leader, and regular jobs to do.

Dogs need a pack. A secure place in the social structure gives them security and self-confidence. Like wolves, dogs need a social community. Without strong ties, sooner or later they will develop behavior problems. Fortunately for people, dogs don't have to have a canine pack; they readily accept human families or even individuals. Whether a large community or a small pack, the togetherness has to work and the pecking order has to be clear—nothing rubs a dog the wrong way more than an "open relationship" where all are free to do as they please.

Dogs need a leader. They want a "boss" they can acknowledge and who will correct them when they go astray. The boss must not be inconsistent, or the dog may be inclined to view that as an invitation to test willpower. All family members must also be firm and consistent with the dog; otherwise, it will make demands of the weaker people that the "top dog" will not grant.

Dogs need duties. Little lapdogs as well as working dogs are glad to have work and duties that they can accomplish.

It's really that simple—but also so difficult, evidently, for this is the root of problems when dogs become disobedient and cause trouble. If you want a happy, obedient dog, you have to come to a mutual understanding; you have to understand the dog and make yourself clearly understood. That's why you have to know the fundamental patterns of dog behavior: You need to know what the dog is trying to tell you vocally and through body language, what development phases the puppy is going through, and why eventual behavior problems are often preprogrammed in puppyhood.

Sounds Dogs Make

Barking. A barking dog invites people and other dogs to play, but barking also serves to defend house and home. Barking is a warning and an alarm. It can serve as a distraction; it often expresses insecurity, anxiety, and

This little dog alertly waits for its handler's instructions.

sometimes aggression. Dogs bark out of boredom and sometimes just to hear their own
voices. There are some characteristic types of
barking that can be clearly distinguished from
others:

✔ Alarm barking: Very loud and unrestrained,
especially when the dog wants to announce a
dangerous or unknown situation.

✔ Barking a warning: A succession of short,
sharp barks, sometimes with short pauses
between, often coupled with threatening
posture (see table on page 11).

✔ Barking to beg: Demanding, often in a high
voice, if some desire is not fulfilled, such as
not receiving an expected treat; persistent,
monotonous, slowed down to medium tempo.

*A dog keeps unknown people and dogs at a
distance by barking a warning.*

✔ Barking at play: Clear and high, often with
pauses, inviting other dogs or people to join in
the play.

✔ Barking a threat: Gruff and low, often mixed
with growling.

Growling. Growling dogs are sending a
warning. They want to keep others from coming too close, taking their bone or toy, or plac-
ing them in a situation for which they're not
prepared.

Aggressive growling is rare. It is clearly dis-
tinguishable from growling out of anxiety or

defense by its intensity and its threatening quality (including threatening posture).

Growling in play-fighting with other dogs or people (such as while playing fetch) is not meant seriously.

Whining. Whining is puppy talk, even when used by adult dogs, especially if they find that it produces the desired effect on humans. Whining signifies submission to humans or to other dogs. It is often accompanied by a meek posture. Its purpose is the appeasement of the other dog or person, sometimes also a gentle attempt to get what it wants. A dog also whines when sick or in pain.

Howling. To the dismay of their owners, many dogs howl when lonely or left alone. The pack-animal dog tries to reestablish voice contact with the family by howling loudly.

Snorting. Air is blown audibly through the nose, usually quickly and forcefully. Snorting is intended to make other dogs or the family aware of an unknown or incomprehensible situation; it can also express displeasure.

Grumbling. Dogs that have been scolded or that are forbidden to bark often try to sneak in the undesirable behavior through repeated, muffled grumbling. Grumbling is a veiled complaint.

Body Language

The body. A dog's body language spans the extremes between appearing huge and becoming invisible. Individual expressions (see table on page 11) can overlap one another or flow easily from one to another. A dog that wants to make an impression has to show size, strength, and self-confidence. Imposing mannerisms include broadening the front part of the body, walking stiff-legged to appear taller, raising the fur in the shoulder and neck area (the hackles), holding the head slightly to the side without staring at the other dog, and holding the tail high.

Checklist
Handling a Puppy

1 Buy a puppy only from a good breeder (see HOW-TO: Getting Started, pages 28–29).

2 Establish a relationship with the puppy through two or three visits before taking it home; that makes the separation from mother and siblings easier.

3 The first days are important in building a relationship: Don't leave the dog alone for very long.

4 Keep the puppy's bed in one place. Don't disturb the dog when it's in bed.

5 The puppy's capacity to learn is at its maximum until about the twentieth week of life. The puppy has to develop trust in you.

6 The principles of early training to avoid bad behavior are: reprimand, distract, and provide alternatives.

7 Don't be overprotective of the young dog.

8 Accustom the puppy to being handled.

In confrontations with stronger antagonists, dogs make themselves small and insignificant. Weight shifted to the hindquarter, tail held low, body turned away, and averted glance indicate submission. In a fight, dogs surrender by demonstrating meekness: They expose the vulnerable throat and belly by lying on their back or side.

Tail. Wagging denotes happiness, but it can also signify concentration on a task. A tail held high shows self-confidence and strength; in that case, wagging shows a friendly disposition; holding the tail stiff signifies defensiveness and a threat. The lower the tail sinks, the more anxious and uncertain the dog is. Dogs that tuck their tails between their legs have no self-confidence. Exceptions are breeds for which that behavior is typical, such as the Whippet.

Facial expression. Many breeds, such as the German Shepherd Dog, have contrasting, expressive facial features. On dogs of just one color, the direction of the hair provides contrast. Different "faces" provide additional expressions.

✔ Threatening: Wrinkling the face and lips; showing the incisors and canine teeth; fixed stare.

✔ Playful expression: "Smiling" by drawing back the corners of the lips and exposing the teeth.

✔ Submission: Drawing the corner of the mouth far to the back.

✔ Anger: Wrinkled snout; piercing and fixed gaze.

Ears. Ears are pointed back to indicate submission, also while fighting; ears held high and pointed to the front indicate alertness, self-confidence, and sometimes a threat. There are, of course, many nuances. With ears that hang down, the mood can be recognized by the muscle movement where the ears join the head.

Further indications. Licking the lips means friendly submission; a nudge with the nose is an invitation to pat or to play; lifting a paw is an attempt to establish contact or reconciliation; a fixed stare indicates interest in something, such as a treat.

*Let's play! This dog's posture—
elbows on floor and hindquarters
raised—shows readiness for a romp.*

Dog Language at a Glance

	Body Language	Sounds	Situation
Friendly and reserved (active submission)	Self-confident manner; head high; ears forward; tail relaxed and low or held high and wagging; occasional eye contact.	None	Contact with other familiar dogs, friendly people, or friends of the owner.
Happy	Erect posture; head high; ears forward; tail high, wagging; eye contact.	Greeting bark	Greeting friends or acquaintances.
Uncertain, expectant	Indecisive; ears slightly laid back; lowered tail; usually no eye contact.	None	Strangers or unknown situation.
Anxious, threatening (defensive threatening)	Tense posture, often ready to bolt; raised hackles; head slightly turned away; teeth bared, sometimes snapping at the air; ears laid back; tail held low; sporadic eye contact.	Uncertain growling, occasional barking	Sudden confrontation with people or other dogs that come upon them in a direct and threatening way.
Self-confident, threatening (attack threat)	Stiff posture; head held high; teeth bared; ears forward; tail high; fixed stare.	None, or warning growl	The dog feels it's master of the situation. If adversary does not flee, attack often follows.
Submissive (passive submission)	Dog tries to appear small. It wants to appease by licking and giving its paw; may urinate; ears back; tail low, often slightly wagging or tucked along side; no eye contact.	None, or whining	The dog has made a mistake and is being admonished; also surrender in dog fights.
Inviting to play	Low front quarters; hindquarters high; some jumps; ears forward; vigorous tail wagging; fixed eye contact.	Loud barking with pauses	Dog wants to urge a person or another dog to play.

INTERPRETING

BEHAVIOR

Dogs communicate with scent signals, body language, and sounds.

 Typical dog behavior, particularly with other dogs

What does this form of body language mean?

How a dog handler should act in such a situation

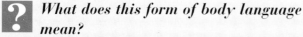 The dog sits in front of you with raised paw and head tipped to one side.

Typical behavior of a dog looking for indulgence or attention.

For training reasons, don't always give in immediately to entreaties and begging.

Two dogs stand nose to nose with tails held high.

First tentative contact between two self-assured dogs that don't know each other.

Give your dog plenty of chances to meet other dogs.

Unrestrained but playful tests of strength.

In play-fighting, dogs develop skills in attacking, defending, and submitting.

Don't interfere! Dogs learn social skills and compatibility by playing.

A male dog lifts his leg and urinates.

It wants to cover over the scent marking of another dog by urinating.

Give the dog an opportunity to sniff and mark on every walk ("reading the news").

With lifted tail the Dalmatian allows another dog to sniff its hind parts.

Scent checking the "anal features" is important for one dog to get to know another dog better.

Allow dogs to greet each other as often as possible without force or leash.

A male dog mounts a standing, receptive female.

Male and female dogs often remain coupled for up to 40 minutes after mating.

Never separate mating dogs or they may injure one another.

The dog lies on its back and exposes its belly to the owner.

Offering the vulnerable underbelly is a gesture of humility and resignation.

As sovereign "top dog," accept the display of submission and pat your dog.

The puppy raises its snout up to its mother's mouth.

Head movement signifies appeasement and request for attention.

Watching the mother dog can provide lots of tips for raising the puppy.

With furrowed brow and bared teeth, this German Shepherd Dog stares at a person or another dog.

Aggressive and threatening, the dog is prepared to attack its opponent.

Immediately distract a leashed dog from the stimulus and give the command "Sit!"

Clear understanding is the basis of living harmoniously with a dog.

What Language Does the Dog Understand?

Dogs are very good at understanding human body language (posture, facial expression, gestures). They are also attentive to voice pitch, tone, and volume and even react to the subtlest changes in scent that humans produce in different situations. That's why it's so important that our spoken commands agree with our body language to prevent misunderstandings. Here's an example of a misunderstanding: When a dog barks at a welcome visitor, its owner pats it and speaks to it in a calming voice. The dog understands that as praise and will bark again in the future.

How Does a Dog Learn?

Dogs learn through experience. They will gladly do anything they relate to a positive experience and avoid anything related to negative experiences.

Therefore, desirable behavior must be reinforced; undesirable behavior must be reprimanded. It's important to react quickly, preferably as the behavior is occurring; otherwise, the dog does not relate the treatment to the behavior.

Don't encourage a dog that jumps up: turn it away.

The Fundamentals of Association

To persuade a dog to react to a command such as "Sit!" you have to use the principle of positive association.

Example: Teaching the dog to sit. A treat is moved from in front of the hungry dog's nose to over its head in such a way that the dog can reach it only by sitting down ("magnetic force"). As it does so, simultaneously give the command "Sit!" and the treat. To keep the dog from getting up right away, pat it and praise it enthusiastically until you end the exercise, for example by saying "Run!" It's important to release the executed command before the dog is free to go.

Hint: Introduce the dog playfully to "Lie down!" "Stay!" and "Come!" by motivating it with treats.

Praise the dog and pat it to keep it in the sitting position for a while.

Encourage Desirable Behavior

Training a dog is a 24-hour proposition. All positive and negative actions by the dog must be praised or scolded; the dog can be influenced only during the momentary action. You can praise your dog with words, pat it, or give it a treat. The important thing is that the dog connect the reward with the right action. Dogs learn best through "positive conditioning"; that is, situations controlled so that the dog naturally does what you want it to. Additional measures include:

✔ Avoid distraction through other stimuli during training games.
✔ Always use the same commands and unmistakable gestures.
✔ Quiet but consistent commands in a firm tone of voice force the dog to be more attentive.
✔ Don't demand too much by giving the dog complicated tasks.
✔ When you want to work on new commands, the duration of the exercise has to be adjusted to the dog's age and attention span.
✔ Choose times for play-training when the dog is active, receptive, and hungry.
✔ You must reinforce commands that the dog has carried out.

Pulling the fur and giving the dog a lecture serves only to make the dog insecure.

How to Correct Bad Behavior

There are several ways to scold a dog effectively for bad behavior.
✔ Often a sharp "No!" works.
✔ Ignore the dog for a while or banish it to its corner.
✔ The "neck bite" can work with thick-haired dogs: Grab ("bite") the dog quickly on the back of the neck and push it downward. Caution: Do not use this training technique with large or dominant dogs unless you are an exprerienced owner-trainer. Never allow children to try this.
Hint: It's totally useless to punish the dog by not feeding it, by locking it up, or by giving it a lecture.

Crouch down and call the dog gently so it comes to you.

WHY DOES A GOOD DOG TURN INTO A PROBLEM DOG?

Our demands on the dog keep increasing: We want a faithful companion in all of life's situations, a partner in sport and play, a friend to the children, a comforter, and a watchdog. The dog's needs are sometimes overlooked. The result: a problem dog.

The Desire for Partnership

Recognizing the problem is half the battle; that's true for many problems and interpersonal crises, both in human relationships and in partnerships between humans and animals. Rarely do major, fundamental faults in the dog's behavior block the way to a smooth relationship between human and dog. It's almost always small oversights and misunderstandings that creep in unnoticed and are accepted and excused until they suddenly cross the threshold of discomfort. Problems that sneak up gradually and on stealthy paws have disadvantages and advantages, namely, the danger of getting used to the wrong role play between human and dog, and the chance to learn from mistakes and turn the training in a new direction by small steps.

Problems with the dog are often rooted in how the puppy was raised. The newborn pup is receptive to and eager for everything. It tests and refines its inherited abilities, it processes countless impressions from its surroundings, and it learns where adjustment is required and where it's empowered to make its own way—at first in the community of the litter, with mother and siblings and in contact with the trainer, and later in the important first phase of life with the new family. It's here that the groundwork is first laid for the sociability and cooperativeness of the young dog. Every dog is endowed with a desire for partnership. Dogs born with inherited behavior defects are rare exceptions. It's the job of the new owner to invite the dog to integrate, without cutting it off from its instinctual needs. In other words, our expectations of the dog should match its expectations of us as much as possible. And that's true not just during puppyhood.

What the Dog Expects from Us

The dog is a social animal. Its inborn need for social contact and its readiness to integrate into a relationship made its domestication possible, but even after nearly 15,000 years of partnership, the dog has not turned into a human child on four feet. A dog has fundamental needs that we need to meet.

Partners in sport and play: A dog is a child's best friend and companion.

✔ Order. The dog needs a secure place in the family structure.

✔ Care. Regular, measured nourishment, health maintenance (regular immunizations and checkups from the veterinarian), care of body and coat.

✔ Activity. Daily exercise of at least 30 minutes; athletic breeds need at least two hours.

✔ Occupation. Directed play with demanding tasks (fetch, obstacles, search).

✔ Social life. Regular contact with other dogs.

✔ Joining in. Going almost every place you do, making acquaintances, having new experiences, such as going on a shopping trip.

✔ Affection and dialogue. Daily affection and intimacy.

✔ Private space. Its own place for resting and sleeping without being disturbed.

Appreciation for the dog is predicated on understanding and knowledge. It's hard for new dog owners to be experts in dog behavior, but they must at least have a desire for community and a readiness to give up

some habits. Dogs change our lives! But dogs are also capable of some astonishing compromises: adjusting their daily rhythm (periods of activity and rest) to that of their human family, learning to suppress specific behavior traits (for example, expecting to be fed in the house, or sleeping in a bed with the pack family), and adjusting to unaccustomed requirements (riding in a car, train, or elevator, staying alone in the house for hours, living happily with other house pets).

What Do You Expect from Your Dog?

Family dogs rarely have a regular job. That distinguishes them from working dogs, which must have specific talents, abilities, and special training. The demands on working dogs are clearly delineated. But even for family dogs there is a catalog of expectations that is in no way inferior to that of working dogs, for today a family dog is expected to be a jack of all trades.

It must be the perfect companion, self-assured but inconspicuous in all situations; it must be a friend and a playmate to the children; it must earn a position in the family as consoler, become a partner in sport and fitness, and be a courageous defender and the rightful guardian of house and home.

This wish list is an expression of a positive development; today, the dog lives with and among the family in an intense and lively way as never before. But the dog cannot meet every demand. You should understand clearly from the outset that a family dog cannot handle all the demands of a companion, watchdog, working dog, and hunting dog. Keep your demands on the dog reasonable as time goes on.

Small training tricks keep the dog busy and strengthen its self-confidence.

Old Dogs and New Tricks

Puppies learn best through the twentieth week of life (their impressionable stage). With adult dogs, a lot more time, energy, and persistence are required to break them of peculiarities and faults. Puppies are born with a desire to learn. Mother Nature sees to that so that they have the chance to become fit for life. Fitness in this case is not only physical, but rather the ability to take in all kinds of experiences and impressions. Fitness assures dogs' survival in the wild. It's not so dramatic with family dogs, whose puppyhood training and experiences determine whether the future will bring harmony or problems. With wolves and wild

Paired fitness jog: Always use a leash in woods and wilderness areas.

dogs, raising puppies is a pack effort; with family dogs, it's a job for the humans.

Mistake Number 1: Starting training too late. People overlook the puppy's transgressions too long: making messes, gnawing, refusing to eat, persistent whining. The result: a spoiled, obstinate young dog. It's therefore important to start basic training within a few days of the dog's arrival in your home. A puppy can and will learn. The trick is positive reinforcement: Praise generously when things go right. If they don't, try again, but never scold! Keep everything fun and playful for both dog and owner.

A Tailor-Made Friend

	The Right Choice
Affection and tenderness	Female dogs are usually more affectionate and gentler than males, but, of course, there ae exceptions.
Obedience	Obedience is based on training and upbringing. Domineering males can be stubborn and test who's the boss. Some hounds and terriers can be stubborn.
Defense and guarding instinct	Airedale Terrier, Doberman Pinscher, German Shepherd Dog, Giant Schnauzer, Kuvasz, Rottweiler, herding dogs and some working dogs.
Sport and leisure partner	All medium-sized dogs that are not too heavy. Best runners: Dalmatian, Greyhound, Setters. Tireless and alert: Border Collie.
Friend to children	Well-balanced breeds such as Beagle, Golden Retriever, Labrador Retriever.
Strength and intimidation	Big, impressive, confident breeds: German Shepherd Dog, Great Dane, Mastiff, Rottweiler, Saint Bernard.
Liveliness	Energetic family members: Border Collie, Cairn Terrier, Chihuahua, Finnish Spitz, Fox Terrier, Jack Russell Terrier.
Cleanliness	Long-haired breeds drag twigs and weeds into the house, but even short-haired dogs shed fur! Least shedding: Airedale Terrier, Bedlington Terrier, Poodle.
Perfect companion	Good candidates include: Bearded Collie, Boxer, Collie, Corgi, Dalmatian, Golden Retriever, Labrador Retriever.
For small apartments	Boston Terrier, Bulldog, Chihuahua, Lhasa Apso, Maltese, Pug, Pekingese, West Highland White Terrier, Miniature Poodle.
As only dog	Bull Terrier, Chow Chow, Doberman Pinscher.
Compatibility with other pets	This works best if the animals are brought up together. Avoid bringing together hunting dogs or ratters and their natural prey.

Ankle biter: A dog that attacks its owner thinks it's the boss.

Mistake Number 2: Overindulgence. Of course a puppy needs watching over, but everything in its time—you decide when it's time to play and how you mix the play with training exercises.

Mistake Number 3: Going too fast. Easy does it; puppies need time to learn. A puppy owner should expect to be on 24-hour call; the new puppy is constantly coming to terms with new stimuli, and especially in the fourth and fifth month of life it needs sympathetic, consistent guidance and direction. The puppy learns all commands (including "Sit!," "Lie Down!," "Stay!," and "Come!") through directed play and positive association (see HOW-TO: Understanding Your Dog, page 14). Always structure the play when the dog is rested and active, and end the game before the dog tires. The dog will then remember the game fondly and repeat it willingly.

Mistake Number 4: Too many teachers. "Too many cooks spoil the broth," and that's true also in puppy training. One family member should be responsible for the training and should train the dog alone; puppies are easily distracted. The other family members can take over the commands later on.

Mistake Number 5: Spoiling. Young dogs that are sheltered too much often don't know how to respond properly to other dogs. A puppy that is picked up by its owner whenever it's frightened by other dogs scarcely has a chance to test its repertory of canine social skills, and it overestimates its abilities.

Four Ground Rules for Togetherness

Let's say someone has an unexpected free day and looks forward to a walk with the dog. But what does the dog do? It begs off and takes another nap. Whether reluctance, rebelliousness, or resistance to commands, a dog's bad behavior is usually the result of a troubled relationship between dog and human.

Respect needs. Your dog's feeding times and naps should be kept sacred. If a dog is roused from a great nap to go and play, that's a setup for it to be ornery and in a bad mood. Dogs develop remarkable finesse in dealing with people who give them senseless commands just for the fun of it, or who annoy them mischievously.

Beware of equal rights. Give them an inch and they'll take a mile. If you concede too much to dogs, they climb up in the pecking order. They don't do it out of spite; it's simply canine nature. In pack and family, a leader is recognized only by being an example for the dog.

Loud is out! Strength (rank) has nothing to do with volume. Dogs react to whispered commands and even to gestures. Dogs that are yelled at wince in fear and experience anxiety. At the first opportunity, an anxiety-ridden dog will steal something or turn on its master.

Maintain a quiet but firm and emphatic tone of voice. Your dog will be obedient and happy to obey.

Hitting never helps. Corporal punishment undermines trust. Trust is the basis for commanding and for obedience. Useful measures for dealing with undesirable behavior are listed in HOW-TO: Understanding Your Dog, on pages 14 and 15.

Typical Traits of Dogs

Young dogs are open to relationships. That's the basis for their becoming lovable partners to people with their varied demands. But dogs have their own past history. Their wolf heritage still dictates character and personality. All dog lovers should carefully consider if they are ready to accept typical behavior patterns as well as breed-specific idiosyncrasies.

Dogs are runners. Even lapdogs need daily exercise. If you don't give a dog a chance for activity, you'll soon have a moody pest in the house.

These dogs pose minimal demands, but still need at least 30 minutes of daily exercise: Basset Hound, Chihuahua, Dachshund, Finnish Spitz, Pug. At least two hours: Dalmatian, Greyhound, Siberian Husky, Setters.

Note: Never let a disobedient and impulsive dog run unrestrained. Keep it on a leash or let it loose only in secure areas. That way there's greater safety in physical movement combined with purposeful activity.

Dogs bark. Even well-trained dogs are not totally silent. More vocal breeds include small, alert ones such as the Chihuahua, Miniature Pinscher, Dachshund, Fox Terrier, Finnish Spitz, and Miniature Schnauzer. The following are quieter by nature: Basset Hound, Bearded Collie, Bernese Mountain Dog, Bull Terrier, Irish Wolfhound, Newfoundland.

Dogs need a pack. The pack can be a whole family, but can also consist of only a human and a dog. Dogs suffer from isolation when they're left alone or separated for too long; they may alter their behavior (by chewing things, for instance) and can become ill.

A litter of pups shares warmth, security, and trust.

Dogs that need closeness include the Boxer, Bernese Mountain Dog, Briard, Pekingese, Poodle, Pug, Shetland Sheep Dog, Siberian Husky, West Highland White Terrier. More independent breeds include the Borzoi, Bulldog, and Great Pyrenees. The Afghan Hound, Chow Chow, Doberman Pinscher, and Saluki can be one-person dogs.

Dogs need a leader of the pack. In the pack the most experienced and self-assured dog prevails. As long as it shows no weakness, it will be accepted by all members. Your dog sees you in precisely that position.

Companionable dogs include the Beagle, Bernese Mountain Dog, Boxer, Golden and Labrador Retrievers, Poodle, Pug, and West Highland White Terrier. Dogs not for beginners are the Akita, Basenji, Doberman Pinscher, Rottweiler, and herding dogs.

The game with endless possibilities: A ball is the favorite toy of many dogs.

Dogs Need Responsibilities

A dog that's cooped up will turn into a bored, unhappy, disobedient nuisance that can suddenly present many problems.

Dogs need to be kept busy. There are plenty of jobs for them: finding and fetching missions, games and play, guarding and protecting, and even work as herding, hunting, or rescue dogs. People who think that only trained working dogs and guard dogs can perform these tasks simply haven't tried with their own dogs. They would be amazed by what the dogs can do!

Sport and games for all. There's no such thing as a totally unathletic dog, and many dogs will even turn their back on their food for a game of ball. Mild play often has a therapeutic effect, for example with senior, convalescent, and pregnant pets.

"Mind sports" keep dogs fit. Combination tasks such as a toy hidden in a box or under a blanket, or a ball that can be retrieved only if the dog uses its smarts, develop the dog's mind and alertness. Particularly cunning breeds are the Border Collie, Finnish Spitz, German Shepherd Dog, Poodle, Smooth and Wire Fox Terriers, and West Highland White Terrier.

Work is fun. A life of luxury is not what dogs want. They are pros, grateful every time they are called on to defend and guard; they pull sleds and milk wagons, follow scents, and herd sheep, cows, and chickens. Watchdogs and work dogs include Boxers, Doberman Pinschers, Great Danes, Rottweilers, and shepherds.

Examples of herding dogs are the Australian Cattle Dog, Bearded Collie, Border Collie, Cardigan Welsh Corgi, and Pembroke Welsh Corgi.

Draft and sled dogs include the Alaskan Malamute, Bernese Mountain Dog, Samoyed, and Siberian Husky.

Breed Characteristics
Most dogs are eager to learn, adaptable, and quick to react, but every breed has its own characteristics. Breeds with two approximately equivalent characterizing features are mentioned twice.

Alert and interested in everything. Border Collie, Boxer, Jack Russell Terrier, Standard Schnauzer, Miniature Pinscher. These breeds are for people who regard partnership with a bundle of energy as a challenge.

Particularly devoted, well-rounded, and good-natured: Basset Hound, Bearded Collie, Irish Wolfhound, Labrador and Golden Retrievers, Newfoundland, Pug, West Highland White Terrier.

Top athletes: Afghan Hound, Borzoi, German Shepherd Dog, Siberian Husky, many terrier breeds, setters. These are absolutely unsuited to life as couch potatoes!

Dogs that need responsibilities and work: Bearded Collie, Border Collie, Briard, German Shepherd Dog, Siberian Husky, retrievers, setters, and dogs that demand attention, affection, and lots of time and energy.

An unmistakable invitation to go out.

Self-assured and fearless: Airedale Terrier, Bull Terrier, Doberman Pinscher, German Shepherd Dog, Kuvasz, Mastiff, Rottweiler, Saint Bernard, Staffordshire Terrier; these dogs need a consistent but gentle guiding hand, and are for experienced owners.

Charming but strong-willed: Akita, Bulldog, Chow Chow, Dachshund, Finnish Spitz, Scottish Terrier, Shiba Inu. For owners who respect dogs with a strong personality (even stubbornness).

Behavior Problems and Their Causes

Mistakes in upbringing, inherited hunting and defense instincts, and boredom and its effects understandably lead to problems with dogs. If you know the cause and the development, undesirable behavior can be remedied quite easily, or at least changed so that it ceases to be a burden on the partnership between human and dog. Real crises in the dog-person relationship come about in two ways: either as an ailment that manifests itself suddenly or as a gradual problem that everyone knows about but that no one takes seriously until it's too late.

Causes of Problems That Come Up Suddenly
✔ A change in the structure of the pack (family): a new mate for the dog owner; the arrival of a baby; change in care and control of the dog because of work demands, illness, death, or vacation; a new pet in the house.
✔ New living or environmental conditions: a move; a change in daily routine, for example as the result of a change in the owner's work hours; different food; a change in play areas and in accustomed routes for walks; a desire to be with dog friends; notification of a new rule around the house (such as not being allowed into the bedroom); a desire for a favorite

TIP

Aptitude Test

Which dog is right for you?
You can recognize typical breed characteristics only by observing adult animals. Check page 28 for what to look for in choosing a puppy.

Big, strong, confident dogs: Can I lead this dog on a leash (applicable to all who will take care of the dog)? Am I consistent enough to stand up to the dog? Am I ready to welcome it into the house?

Herding dogs, Greyhounds, and working dogs: Do I have energy and time to give the dog enough to do, plus ample daily exercise? Is someone there at all times to take it for training behind a bicycle or at the dog track (Greyhounds, for example)?

One-person dogs, companion dogs, and small dogs: Can my dog regularly accompany me to the office or on leisure activities? What will I do with the dog during vacation or when I'm sick?

Dogs requiring special attention: Am I ready to invest time in brushing (usually daily for long-haired dogs) and time and money for clipping or trimming? Anyone interested in a spotlessly clean house can expect to have problems.

Important: Do I have the consent of the people I live with and/or the landlord to keep a dog?

The look that says "I want to go too!"

plaything; frequently being left alone; competition with a dominant or aggressive dog in the living quarters; a receptive female dog in the vicinity; continuous disturbance during periods of rest and sleep.

Causes of Problems That Gradually Creep Up
  Lack of exercise and activity; excessive pampering and sheltering; subtle or obvious increase in aggressive behavior by the dog handler toward people or other dogs; insufficient social contact with other dogs; owner's indulgence at feeding time or with a begging dog; continuous favoritism of the dog with respect to family members; other dogs or additional pets in the house; traumatic experiences while riding in the car or lack of adjustment to the car; lack of subordination training (domineering behavior); neglect (possible lack of housebreaking).

The Right Accessories
  Some problems with dogs arise because people don't have the right equipment to train and handle them. Note the following:
  Collar: The collar should be of strong but flexible material (preferably leather or synthetic), and it must cover at least two neck

vertebrae. It must also fit in such a way that the dog can't slip it off. Choke or slip collars should be avoided in positive rearing and training.

Leash: Leather (strong, especially for strong dogs), nylon (for small to medium-size dogs), Flexi (extendable, giving dogs that aren't allowed off the leash a little room to roam), even a light-reflecting leash.

Grooming accessories: Brush and comb without sharp edges or teeth.

Food and water dishes: Spillproof, taste-free, unbreakable.

Bed: Washable blankets and cushions, and placed in a draft- and disturbance-free location.

Transportation crate: Matched to your dog's size; stable, windproof, gnawproof.

Toys: Made of soft plastic with no metal core; medium-sized so they can't be swallowed; free of chemicals and dyes.

When Do I Need Help from a Professional?

Experts in dog training have experience with difficult dogs. A dog training course is recommended if:

✔ a problem lasts for a long time (about six months or longer)

✔ the dog becomes dangerous (tendency to bite, continued straying)

✔ you have to admit that your patience and energy are exhausted

Checklist
What Are Your Dog's Symptoms?

A dog's obvious and typical behavior traits can usually be directly connected to specific problems. A thorough analysis of the most common problems starts on page 33.

1 Listless, apathetic behavior: Grieving dogs; loss of vitality and old age; withdrawal and timidity; nocturnally active dogs; anxiety at being left alone.

2 Resistance, rebelliousness, and disobedience: Lack of confidence; indulgence by owner; jealousy; lack of attention; excessive impulsiveness; altered family structure; lost love; being left alone too frequently and for too long.

3 Obtrusiveness, nagging: Excessive pampering; indulgence by owner; lack of attention.

4 Dominance to the point of snapping: Unclear human/dog hierarchy.

Choosing a Puppy

If possible, visit the puppies often to find the one whose character shows the most promise. Here are the basics:

✔ Puppies that cower in the corner often remain shy and timid.

✔ Puppies that immediately nip every visitor or try to get their way by biting need firm training and are not suited to beginners.

✔ The ideal: Puppies that submit willingly without showing anxiety. They come wagging their tails, are happy to be patted, and want to lick your hand.

This puppy comes running happily when called.

How to Find the Right Breeder

Get addresses from the American Kennel Club (see page 62).

✔ Get advice from an experienced breeder or veterinarian on breed-specific behavior traits for your desired dog.

✔ Good breeders will ask you lots of questions to get to know you better. They almost give the impression that they'd rather keep their puppies.

✔ The dogs have family ties and are kept in the pen only an hour at a time.

✔ They demonstrate interest in visitors, confidence, and friendliness, and are neither anxious nor aggressive.

✔ Sleeping quarters and food bowls are clean.

✔ From the fourth week of life on, you can visit the puppy regularly; this is an important step in getting it used to you.

✔ The breeder gives you tips on care and feeding for the first weeks at home.

This puppy trusts you to pick it up in your arms.

✔ The breeder maintains regular contact with you after you have taken the pup home.

✔ Papers and shot records are complete. The puppy's registration papers are subsequently furnished, as provided in the sales agreement.

This puppy acts anxious and remains sitting when called.

Obedience Classes

To foster a puppy's healthy development, it is recommended that you and your pup attend good dog obedience classes. The puppy will learn there with others the same age how to behave among dogs; you will be able to assess its strength and abilities and help it develop confidence. Dogs that are denied these social games with other dogs will be timid or won't know how to behave properly.

How to Deal with Problems

Your veterinarian is the first person to contact about all problems. Before treatment, the veterinarian will have to ascertain that a particular behavior is not caused by health problems.

Dog psychologists or dog therapists treat their patients one-on-one at home in their accustomed surroundings.

Treatment of a dog that has undesirable behavior is possible only when the causes of the problem are eliminated. Since the causes usually are found in the dog's immediate surroundings (improper treatment, for instance), it makes sense in many cases to keep the dog owner involved from the very beginning of therapy.

Dogs and their owners practicing in training classes.

Systematic Training

Dog obedience classes offer more than special instruction for problem dogs. People who have limited experience with dogs can enjoy regular training and playtime with their pets, so handing the dog over to a training program by itself makes sense only if you have learned how to handle your dog properly by the end of a basic course.

In a good dog training class, you don't just learn how to handle your dog properly; you also get a detailed training program based on theory.

BEHAVIOR PROBLEMS AND SOLUTIONS

Most problems with dogs are homemade. They come up in the partnership between human and dog, especially where excessive or false expectations and demands are placed on the dog.

Why Dogs Cause Problems

Healthy alertness and healthy cautiousness are part of a dog's innate behavior. Here we're concerned only with heightened aggression and overanxiety, the most common traits of problem dogs. Both can be inborn, but more often are brought about by unfortunate experiences with people.

Treatment is often difficult because the symptoms overlap one another: Anxiety can lead to defensive aggression; readiness to attack can be brought about by fear.

Causes of Aggressive Behavior

Aggressiveness is always triggered by a specific situation (stimulus).

✔ With strangers: Manifested by excessive staring at visitors; territorial defense behavior encouraged by the owner; unpleasant past experiences.
✔ With the family: Faulty subordination; repeated disturbances while sleeping or eating; pain for some reason that must be investigated.

The Gatekeeper: This alert dog is protecting its house and yard, but it must learn the difference between friends and strangers.

✔ With specific family members: Jealousy; defense of a particular person; unpleasant past experiences.
✔ With other dogs: Excessive competition among male dogs; defensive role (on owner's behalf); insufficient socialization in development phases (lack of contact with other dogs); unpleasant past experiences.

Causes of Anxiety

✔ With strangers: Contact deficit or unpleasant past experiences.
✔ With other dogs or particular breeds: Unpleasant meetings; fights; carryover of owner's anxiety.
✔ With unknown situations, objects, noise, or strange sounds: Insufficient training in puppyhood; excessive pampering by owner.

Further Causes of Behavior Problems

Excessive spoiling, pampering, and protecting make for picky eaters, obtrusive "lap dogs," malingerers, and barkers. Faulty bonding of dog to family produces whining, rebelliousness, destructiveness, disobedience, and biting.

Assault on a pillow: Destructiveness is often the result of being left alone too long.

Trust Is the Foundation for Training

Dogs need recognition; they want to please their owner and they want to be taken seriously and to be members of the family. Praise and positive reinforcement encourage loyalty, obedience, and willingness to cooperate. Each training lesson should end with praise, especially with a young dog.

Training programs that work for puppies and grown dogs also make sense for problem dogs. Many of them have never experienced (or have lost sight of) recognition by a human, which is so necessary for the social creatures that dogs are. Other dogs get attention that doesn't correspond to their needs, or merely reflects the one-sided needs of the owner. For all these dogs, kind talking to and a generous measure of recognition are vital. Dogs that misbehave because they've been denied praise and affection for a long time understandably will respond slowly at first. The following analyses of problems describe situations and causes, as well as how a person can reestablish trust and closeness step by step, even with a supposedly hopeless case.

Misunderstandings

If people don't understand the behavior of their dog, or if they interpret it incorrectly, misunderstandings result. Many of them stem from carelessness that's been tolerated too long. Even if the problem is recognized, it's often hard to fix. Treatment always involves rigorous work with the dog, and review, if necessary. If the solution doesn't go according to plan, the lesson or exercise must be repeated, perhaps with other learning aids, in a new setting or simply when you and your dog are having fun with the training again.

Fear of Being Left Alone

Situation. A dog that's been left alone howls, whines, or barks continuously and/or damages the furniture.

Cause. Dogs, as pack animals, perceive being left alone as punishment, since they feel excluded from society. Being left alone can also cause dogs anxiety because they think they've been left forever. Behind that feeling often lurks insufficient trust in the owner. Howling is intended to restore community by voice contact. Dogs that are left alone often become increasingly destructive.

Remedy. The best way for a dog to develop trust for its master is through gradual training. At first, leave the dog alone in a room for just a short while—about a minute—while you stay in a different room. Don't stand right in front of the door, since dogs have good hearing. If the dog howls or barks, go into the room calmly and without speaking, and reprimand with the neck bite (see HOW-TO: Understanding Your Dog, pages 14–15). If necessary, throw a chain collar or tin can onto the floor as a noise deterrent, then immediately leave the room without further contact.

Later, increase the separation time little by little; shorten it again in case of relapse.

Helpful measures: Tire the dog out physically before leaving it alone (play and romp energetically), and feed it; a full belly makes a dog sleepy.

Distraction can be helpful (chew bones, guarding a handbag or article of clothing, quiet background music, or a favorite toy). Suggestion: Leave the house without ceremony so that the dog doesn't know you've gone. Upon returning, greet the dog warmly.

Important: Puppies up to the sixteenth week of life shouldn't be left alone more than a half-hour at a time. Closeness to their pack is vital to the development of their personality.

Hint: Length of treatment for puppies will be two to three months, and somewhat longer, with more setbacks, for older dogs.

Panic in the Car

Situation: Many dogs whine, tremble, or get sick while riding in the car. Others defend the car with fang and claw.

This lonely puppy is howling for its human companion.

Cause: Often the fault goes back to the puppy's ride from the breeder to the new family: the rocking of the car, strange people, new sounds, no mother or siblings—everything can add up to produce a scaredy-cat. If the dog is not taught to lose its fear of the car, the fear becomes stronger than its trust in its owner.

Overzealous watchdogs, on the other hand, perceive the car as a first-class territory and defend it with every means at their disposal, believing they're performing a labor of love for their owners.

Solution: Scaredy-cats need to learn that the car is part of the territory in which they live. Regularly sit in the back seat of the parked car with your dog for fairly long periods—at least 30 minutes. Talk to the dog, pat it, give it treats or its favorite blanket or toy. After the dog has gotten used to that, idle the motor in park; later, take short rides while a second person comforts the dog. Increase the duration of the trips. Put the dog in its hard-sided travel crate. It will be safer and will feel comfortable in its own "den."

Distractions for barking dogs: chewing on a bone or a toy; cuddling. Small dogs belong on the floor of the passenger's seat, where they can't see out. Tip: Have a second person walk by the car while you calm the dog or distract it inside. On longer trips, take a break every two hours for a short walk and offer the dog a drink of water.

If you let your dog take over the place where you and your family sit, it will think it rules the roost and you'll have a difficult time training it.

Dogs that are sensitive to the movement of the car should be able to look out the window, and can even be given travel pills for nausea (available from the veterinarian). The last feeding should be about three hours before the trip. Always keep water handy.

If proper trust is established, even the most nervous dogs will soon become pleasant travel companions. In the case of super-watchdogs and barkers, the outlook for success is less promising since they are defending not only their mobile territory, but also their owner. For a while, perhaps only friends and acquaintances will be able to ride with the dog. In extreme cases, professional help in car training at dog obedience classes may help.

Feeding Problems

Situation: A dog's stubborn food preferences become an ongoing problem for many owners.

Cause: Dogs are basically fast eaters. With excessive gulpers, professional jealousy often plays a role—for example, because of another dog, a different house pet, or lack of trust in the owner. Relationship problems often lurk behind feeding problems. Dogs are quick to notice that they can manipulate their owners through long-term refusal or holding out for particular types of food.

Solution: Obesity is dangerous to heart, circulation, and joints for dogs, which are naturally athletic. Overweight adult dogs should be fed twice daily with the proper amount of high-fiber, low-calorie food. This keeps the dog from becoming ravenously hungry. Apart from mealtimes, the dog should get treats only as a reward; for example, to reinforce its obedience in a training lesson. Dogs don't beg if people don't give them anything. They become poor eaters if food is constantly in their bowl. If the dog walks off, take the food away. Competition for food—such as a second dog at the bowl—can give confirmed poor eaters better appetite.

Note: Refusal to eat can also be an indication of tooth and jaw problems. Consult the veterinarian.

Important: Many dogs defend their food even from the owner. Lack of trust is usually the cause. You shouldn't bother a dog while it's eating. However, if your puppy or dog seems to be choking on its food, you should be able to take the bowl away for a minute and then give it back. In the meantime, pat and calm the dog so that the dog understands that it can trust you and that its food is in no danger. If the dog tries to bite you, coax it away with morsels from the bowl. Then take the bowl away, praise the dog, and return the food.

TIP

The Pecking Order

It starts innocently enough and everybody finds it amusing: The puppy snaps at the owner's hand and growls like a grown-up. For us, that looks like typical puppy play, and the young dog is often encouraged to do it. But it's different for the puppy—it's testing its social status. In the dog's estimation, people who let themselves get bitten, willingly give up the sofa, or are afraid to take away the chew toy deserve no leadership role. What's more, it's absolutely legitimate for dogs to reprimand pack members of a lower rank.

Testing the pecking order is a function of the dog's inherited role awareness. This is not bad behavior, so punishment is not appropriate; however, you should remedy it effectively. In such cases you can put the "neck bite" to good use: The hand seizes ("bites") the puppy quickly in the neck area, accompanied by a strong "No!" or "Bad dog!" The dog will lie down and become docile. Remember: Don't use this too often or it will lose its effectiveness.

Stressful Situations with Play-Actors

Situation: Sudden limping if you start to take the dog out in the rain; trembling all over; whining; lethargic movement when you have to visit the veterinarian; spinning and rolling to get attention.

Checklist
A Dog's Wish List

1 **Variety and stimulation**
An unfamiliar place, a different route for a walk (sometimes even the other side of the street), exciting contacts with other dogs, new scents and sounds. A dog that experiences many different things is a happy dog and a dog that is always enthusiastic.

2 **Sniffing pleasure**
Anyone who thinks that restrained movement is the best thing for a dog is greatly mistaken—a dog also needs time to explore the world thoroughly with its nose. It uses its nose to read a great number of pieces of information. Dogs that are always made to trot beside the owner's bicycle or walk at heel at all times are unfortunate dogs indeed.

3 **Playtime**
Play is extremely important to dogs of all ages. It allows them to blow off steam, gauge their strength, and test their fitness. Dogs strengthen the bonds of harmony by playing with people.

Cause: Many dogs have learned that acting gets them what they want. The desired action usually follows immediately (abandoning a demand, patting, treats) and confirms their role play.

Remedy: Actors that no one notices give up their careers. For good measure, have your dog examined by the veterinarian and, if it's healthy, you'll find it easier to be tough. Then always praise the dog when it has completely settled down again.

Advice: Ignoring a dog's theatrical performances usually produces the desired result.

Dangerous Grief

Situation: A dog loses its owner through sickness, death, or regulations against keeping pets. It reacts with denial, becomes apathetic, and practically ceases to eat.

Cause: For many dogs the loss of its owner means the end of their world. The hierarchy is undone and the safety of the pack has vanished.

Solution: The dog needs lots of distraction and activity. Take it on a walk to new places where it can meet other dogs. Apathy can make a dog give up entirely. If the dog doesn't eat, put its food envy to the test by allowing another dog at the bowl, and move the dog to different surroundings where it's not continually reminded of its owner.

Advice: Patiently and repeatedly offer the dog opportunities to do fun things, and you've practically won the battle. If you revive the dog's spirit, there is only a slim chance of a relapse.

Is There a Cure for Straying?

Situation: Most dogs are escape artists and will run off at every opportunity. Straying dogs endanger themselves and others.

Cause: The passion for straying is especially deep-seated in hunting dogs. Even big dogs tend to stray if their desire for activity is not satisfied. Also, dogs that are bored and have too little to do will stray, as will females in heat and lovesick males.

Solution: Enclose your yard with a fence so the dog can't get out. Spend special playtime with your dog. Have it guard the house, and give it a toy and a chew bone. Start by training the puppy, at first on a long leash—call once, then hide behind a tree or crouch down. Never run after the dog! Also note that you should never let your dog run free in the woods.

The leash and a closed door can help combat the dog's will to roam. Also, spaying females may eliminate the desire to roam. Neutering male dogs is recommended to curb their interest in running after females in heat.

Note: If the dog gets lost in the woods, contact the authorities, search on familiar trails, and set out a comforting object such as a sweater or a blanket to try to lure the dog home.

No More Mounting!

Situation: Male dogs often take every opportunity to mount a person's leg.

Cause: Male dogs that are reared in isolation often are sexually confused and have an aversion to female dogs, but mounting a person's leg is also a show of power—the dog perceives the person as inferior. Among dogs, mounting can be used without sexual connotations. In such cases, it is an aggressive behavior pattern, usually intended to provoke an opponent. Females asserting dominance do this also.

Solution: Turn away abruptly with a sharp "Bad Dog!" or "No!" Distract the dog with a game or leave the dog alone in the room. Don't shake off the offending dog, since that only leads to more intense action. Only the person involved should scold the dog. If someone else pulls the dog off, the dog sees the first person as weak.

When a dog mounts a person's leg, it's a clear gesture of dominance.

Common Mistakes in Training Puppies

All too often puppies get absolutely no training, which has nothing to do with negligence on the part of the owner. Appearances are deceptive with the puppy; sleeping, playing, and eating seem to be its only interests. But that's a false impression—by its seventh week, the puppy's development turns a bit stormy. If you fail to provide it with stimulation and help in development and motivation, you jeopardize the future partnership between dog and human.

Stages in a Puppy's Development

✔ Third to sixth week: Early socialization in the company of littermates; diminishing need for exclusive bond with the mother. Visual perception improves (eyes have been open from the second or third week of life), and the ears open. First milk teeth: transition from pure milk diet to dog food.

✔ Sixth to tenth week: First explorations of surroundings; early play to determine rank among siblings. The pup, naturally reluctant to soil the living quarters, follows the scent trail to the area used by its dam to urinate and defecate. During weaning, the mother leaves the dog bed more frequently and for longer times. Until about the seventh week, puppies run up to people, but starting with the eighth they change their behavior and become more standoffish, especially with strangers.

✔ By the tenth week, the pup has already started to test its abilities and skills. Owners must discourage attempts to bite and chew.

✔ Tenth to twentieth week: Learning stage. The puppy is now of basic schooling age and is particularly impressionable by outside stimuli of all kinds.

✔ From the eighth to the twelfth week: Early training; housebreaking; developing confidence with collar and leash; assignment to resting area.

✔ Starting with the twelfth week: Playful exercises can be started for basic obedience: "Sit!," "Down!," "Heel!," and "Come!"

✔ Sexual maturity (depending on breed, seventh to ninth month for females, ninth to twelfth for males): End of puppyhood. With some breeds, specific instincts, such as guarding and defending, blossom only after two or three years.

✔ At the time of sexual maturity many dogs become moodier, display a tendency to wander, resist commands, or act high-strung and nervous. This stage requires lots of attention and firmness on the part of the owner.

Minor Youthful Offenses

Situation: The puppy nips at shoes and socks, tugs at pants, bites, licks everyone, mounts everyone, and chases birds and cats. The catalog of puppy offenses is long.

Chewing: The pup must learn early what is forbidden.

Cause: The young dog is looking for attention and testing its limits; it wants to fit in and find its position in the new social structure.

Solution: A puppy should never be punished for being curious and active. At the same time, a pup must be trained to be obedient and consistent so it doesn't turn into a problem dog. Determine clearly who is in charge of raising, feeding, and caring for the dog. Puppies are quick to discover if someone in the family is particularly indulgent.

✔ Play biting: Biting hands, legs, pants, and shoes is taboo! But pushing away may be understood as a challenge to bite more, and corporal punishment can lead to destructiveness or defensive aggression. Instead, steer the pup toward activity with toys that are appealing to chew, which also eases teething discomfort.

"Is this okay?" This pup looks at its human to see if it's allowed on the bed.

✔ Hunting games: Young dogs chase birds and cats. If a person expresses approval, the dog feels justified and will become a repeat offender. At any time, the play can turn into real hunting, so it's best to put a stop to any tendency to chase other animals. If the dog is on a leash, give short, strong tugs and reprimand with an energetic "No!" Never pull back on the leash; otherwise, the dog connects returning with reprimand. If the dog is not on a leash, use the "neck bite" (if you are an experienced adult—see page 15) and the command "No!" If the dog had already run away, don't run after it or yell. Walk in the

──────── T I P ────────

Success through Distraction

Puppies are more easily distracted than adult dogs. While mild distractability is undesirable during obedience training, it brings some advantages in dealing with problems—often puppies cease their undesirable behavior in response to an appealing invitation to do something else, at first temporarily, and for longer periods with repetition. It is important to note that the distraction is effective only if offered at the moment the problem behavior occurs. At any other time, it has the opposite effect and is perceived as a reward.

✔ Barking: Distract with chew toys or a game such as fetch.

✔ Making messes: Provide a favorite plaything in rest area. (The bed will practically never be dirtied.)

✔ Biting: Offer chew toys for chewing and biting.

opposite direction or hide behind a tree. Don't scold the dog upon its return, but greet it warmly.

✔ Licking: This is a gesture of friendship and meekness, but not everyone likes it. Reduce displays of affection to limited quantities without rejecting the dog. Distract it with a chew toy.

✔ Mounting: Even young dogs use the leg embrace as a power demonstration (see page 37). Distraction and regular association with other dogs bring improvement.

✔ Begging: Feed the dog only in its bowl—never from the table!

Advice: Patting makes sense for praise and reward only if not overused. Be sparing with reprimands (see also HOW-TO: Understanding Your Dog, pages 14–15).

Anxiety Makes Puppies Sick

Situation: Holding back in unfamiliar surroundings and with strange people spares puppies from unpleasant experiences, but too much caution interferes with their development. The result is timid, nervous biters.

Cause: Traumatic experiences (getting bitten, shots from the veterinarian, noise, a fall on the stairs); a person's excessive caution; a transfer of anxiety from the dog's mother or owner.

Remedy: Unpleasant incidents in puppyhood can mark the dog's entire life. For that reason, it's important not to avoid an anxiety-causing situation altogether, but to give the puppy an opportunity to have new, positive experiences.

✔ Getting bitten: The puppy that is bitten needs immediate contact with other dogs, preferably of the same breed as the biter. That way it learns that not all dogs are mean.

✔ Veterinarian: Set up an appointment outside regular visiting hours, while the waiting room is empty, so that the dog can get to know the doctor in a relaxed atmosphere.

✔ Noise: Don't leave the dog alone on a noisy holiday such as New Year's Eve or the Fourth of July. Pat it and distract it, but don't show pity. To acclimate the pup, expose it to noise (quiet at first, later loud and shrill), and immediately reward it. The connection between noise and reward stops panic reaction fairly quickly.

✔ Fear of stairs: Never pull the dog forcefully on the stairs. Always go first and coax the dog; if necessary, put some treats on the steps.

A small puppy nervously approaches a big Rottweiler. Note the submissive posture.

✔ Excessive spoiling: These animals feel secure only in the immediate vicinity of their humans; they may bark and bite from fear. Allow puppies to associate freely with other dogs. Even if many interactions between dogs appear rough, 99 percent of the time they are harmless. Very sheltered dogs often cannot take advantage of new freedom and hide behind their owner due to anxiety transfer. Dogs can feel when their owners are afraid for them. Only when that is overcome can dogs develop self-confidence.

What Can Be Done about Making Messes?

Situation: Despite all efforts, a puppy forgets the house training it was taught (see House Training Strategy, page 45).

Cause: In the case of persistent messes, have the dog examined by a veterinarian. Assuming there is no underlying physical reason, there may be several causes:
✔ Protest: Change of food; jealousy; frequent absence of the owner; a change in daily routine; repeated disturbances while resting; lack of affection.
✔ Stress: Disturbance and noise in the house and family; move to a strange apartment or surroundings; competition with other pets.
✔ Complete submission to people or other dogs: The dog dribbles urine; likewise when it is excited or happy to see someone again.

Remedy: In the case of protest, eliminate the cause; establish a regular daily routine; enjoy some activities together. A new family member must earn the dog's good will one step at a time (by taking it for a walk, brushing it, or feeding it, for example). If a baby comes into the house, devote even more time to the dog than before. A dog withstands stress better if it's sure of its owner's affection.

New situations and contact with unknown people and dogs develop self-confidence in timid dogs.

Struggling with the Leash

Situation: Many dogs strain against the leash; every walk becomes a test of strength for the owner.

Cause: Faulty, delayed, or nonexistent leash training.

Remedy: At first, merely put the collar on the dog several times a day. Pat the dog; never scold it. During the first walks, be sure that the dog neither plays with the leash nor chews on it. Gradually set the pace and direction through motivation (treats) and clapping your thigh ("Come!"). If the dog pulls too hard, stand still. The length of the leash communicates your wishes to the dog: A short leash means to heel; a long leash means the dog can sniff around to its heart's desire. Retractable leashes are not useful for training because their unrolling makes it harder to influence the dog directly.

Dealing with Thieves

Situation: The dog steals everything that's edible, that belongs to the owners, or that smells like them.

Cause: The desire to pilfer shoes or sweaters is rooted in the first days of puppyhood when carrying off things was permitted. Food thieves are usually opportunists.

Early training should include getting the dog used to collar and leash.

Remedy: If you let the dog steal old shoes, but not new slippers; how's your pet supposed to figure it out? All personal items of the owner must be taboo for the puppy; otherwise, chewing is preprogrammed. Neutral substitutes don't help much, since the only thing that counts is what belongs to the owner.

Avoid giving meat, cheese, and cake thieves an opportunity; clear away foods or lock them up. If that's too much trouble, try the "fright cure": On the edge of the table place some treats to which an empty tin can has been attached. If the dog tries to grab the treats, the can falls to the floor and makes a loud noise. People should stay out of sight so that the dog doesn't link the action to them.

The pack animal dog must learn to be alone from time to time.

Snappers and Cowards

Owners who shelter their puppies too much will soon have a nipper for a partner. The pup will react aggressively in their presence, but away from them it will be a coward. After the puppy has had its shots, let it off the leash to play in areas away from traffic. Grown dogs are almost always tolerant even of mischievous puppies. In any case, reprimands by other dogs are an important part of growing up. **Note:** Starting in the seventh to the eighth week, puppies often run away from strangers. Be sure not to encourage this habit.

Staying Alone without Howling

Leave the pup alone several times a day, but only for a couple of minutes at a time. That works best right after a fairly long walk. If it keeps quiet, give lots of praise when you return, and gradually extend your absences. If the pup howls, burst through the door and scold with "Quiet!" or "Sit!," then leave again. To calm the dog, feed it before you leave, give it a favorite toy (as a reward only at specific times), play a radio softly, or put a hot water bottle under its blanket.

Opportunity Makes Thieves

Even pups steal out of boredom, or because they want to have a paw in everything the family does. Cure boredom with alternative activities, such as sports, games, and combination tasks.

The pup searches single-mindedly for a hiding place for its booty.

Pulling on the Leash

Puppies that pull on the leash usually want to get quickly to interesting places. The more the owner applies the brakes on the other end of the leash, the harder the dog pulls. Here's a helpful solution: immediately stand still when the dog pulls too much. Don't move until the dog understands that pulling does not produce the desired result. Repeat regularly. Also, it's important that the puppy be allowed to romp as much as possible beforehand so it's more willing to go on the leash.

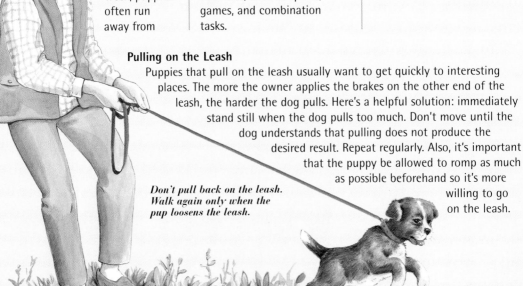

Don't pull back on the leash. Walk again only when the pup loosens the leash.

As much as possible, avoid providing opportunities to steal. You need to pay particular attention to thieves of sweaters, socks, and shoes. For them, scolding is a form of attention and is therefore inappropriate as a cure. Catch the culprit red-handed and distract it with play or small talk. Never look for vanished objects in the company of the puppy; it will like the excitement and steal again.

Puppy Bites Hurt

Chew toys (of chewable rubber, hard plastic, or reconstituted rawhide, impossible to swallow) distract the puppy from biting hands and legs. Control the puppy with "No!" Don't push it away since that

Mouthing in play can develop into biting.

will be perceived only as an invitation to play. At first, keep shoes and other objects hidden away. Squirt stubborn biters with a water pistol.

Don't scold the puppy if an accident has already happened.

to the door; always use the same door to the outside. Usually the puppy becomes restless when it needs to eliminate. Choose an out-of-the-way area. At the beginning, place some of the puppy's own droppings in that spot.

Young dogs forget themselves when they are excited (for example, when they're happy to see someone again or when they meet another dog). That improves as the dog reaches sexual maturity. If need be, greet the dog only after it has calmed down, at which time it's permissible to pat it.

Demonstration of Affection without Licking

Carefully discourage excessive licking. If a person takes charge, a dog holds still and enjoys it. If the dog jumps up or tries to lick your face, push gently on its back with one hand as you pat it. Command "Sit!" and pat the dog only when it has calmed down. After a short time it will connect polite behavior with patting. It's inappropriate to knee a dog that jumps up, or to step on its paws, because these actions may hurt the dog and will instill fear.

House Training Strategy

Your house or apartment are taboo for the puppy's elimination needs; you must show it the way outdoors. After every feeding and sleep time, take the puppy

Discourage the dog early from jumping into people's faces and licking them.

Problems with Canine Nature

Dogs are runners. They are pleased to fit into society, but they continually test the hierarchy. They are hunters and take off after animals that lead them on a chase. They protect their territory and defend packmates. Dogs know how to impress other dogs or give them their marching orders. Dogs have a strong concept of love. They are also attentive and intelligent partners with people and can adapt their behavior to various situations. Dog reality lies somewhere between persisting in their basic nature and integrating into the family. How far the pendulum swings one way or the other depends on demands from both sides, mutual understanding, and on the dog's breed.

Which Breed Is Right for You?

There are more than 400 dog breeds. They are differentiated by body structure, hair color, type of hair, and by character and temperament—every breed brings basic traits to the relationship with humans.

The first exploratory visits to mother and pups (from the fourth week on) show which one of the litter was born to be boss and which ones are shy and retiring (see Choosing a Puppy, page 28). Since you can't yet recognize breed-specific characteristics, you should do the following before you buy a pup:

✔ Get some advice from an independent expert who's a good trainer of all breeds. That person should have no vested interest in your purchasing a specific dog. Draw up a list of positives and negatives: What do you expect from your dog? What would you find annoying?

✔ Read professional literature in professional periodicals or from breed associations.

✔ Establish contact with a veterinarian who can give you valuable hints on care and owning special breeds and advise you on the first weeks with the puppy.

No Closed Season for Hunters

Situation: As soon as the dog glimpses a wild animal or sees the neighbor's cat, it takes off like a shot, resulting in arguments with neighbors and wildlife officials. If a dog is running loose in the woods, in some places it can be legally shot.

Cause: At around six months, a dog's hunting urge awakens. That can lead to problems with hunting dogs and other active breeds. Dogs roam and hunt out of boredom, too (see page 37).

Solution: With dogs that have an inherent love of hunting, you have to assert your authority early, such as before the sixth month of life, by means of consistent basic training. You have to offer grown hunting dogs distraction through sport and play away from their hunting territory, thus providing an outlet for pent-up energy. Combination games and hiding

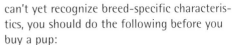

The Saint Bernard has a strong guarding and protecting instinct.

games strengthen obedience and awaken new interests in your dog.

A dog bred to hunt belongs in the hands of an expert hunter.

Training to Suppress the Hunting Urge
✔ Whenever the dog takes off after an animal and your "Stop!" has no effect, quickly hide behind a tree. The dog will soon be at your side, as it is afraid to be suddenly left alone.
✔ With decoys on a rope, intentionally provoke the urge to hunt. Reward every hesitation and every time the dog comes back willingly. Simultaneously offer an appealing distraction such as playing with a ball. Beagles, Fox Terriers, Irish Setters, and Siberian Huskies need particularly consistent training.
Hint: Training to suppress hunting works well with young dogs; with older dogs, the desire is often so deep-seated that repeat offenders are

almost the rule. With sight-hunting dogs such as Afghan Hounds and Borzois, therapy is of no use. Running free off the leash is rarely possible with these dogs, unless you live near a large fenced area such as a dog park or school-grounds where dogs are allowed.

Aggressive Watchdogs
Situation: The dog defends house and yard against everyone, often in the presence of its owner.
Cause: Territorial behavior is inborn in dogs. Normally, the dog handler determines which visitors are welcome. Dogs take over this role

if the handler shows no leadership qualities, or if they must make a decision in the absence of their owner. Overzealous watchdogs can also be dogs that have no designated territory of their own, such as places for resting or sleeping.

Solution: Assuming that the rank order is correct, a simple "Stop!" should suffice to call the dog back. Show the dog that the visit is welcome. Don't leave any dog in the yard without supervision if it has a strong watch instinct (Doberman Pinschers, Finnish Spitzes, German Shepherd Dogs, Great Danes, Rottweilers, terriers). Special watchdogs need their own territory; otherwise, they will defend house and yard as if it all belonged to them. **Hint:** As long as there are no obedience problems and the owner is not secretly proud of the watchdog (since dogs pick up on even unintentional desires), territorial behavior is acceptable. In any case, the dog is not likely to give up its job as watchdog.

Gatekeeper: Overzealous and noisy watchdogs scare away all visitors.

Is Your Dog the Boss?

Situation: Everything revolves around the dog, and all its wishes are fulfilled—at first out of affection, later often out of fear because it gets its way by growling and biting.

Cause: Dogs perceive your indulgence as weakness and take over the dominant position.

Solution: Dogs feel comfortable only in a definite rank within the family; they need a clear structure with commands, obedience, and firmness. Breeds that like to be boss include Akitas, Basenjis, Chow Chows, Doberman Pinschers, and Rottweilers.

People who can't cope with their dogs should attend dog obedience school. If there are hierarchy problems, a training regimen that requires the presence of the owner is recommended (see Obedience Classes, page 29).

Results of Jealousy

Situation: There's a new baby or life partner in the home, which necessarily produces a change in the family structure. Affection and caresses are divided differently and the family dog suddenly becomes an outcast.

Cause: Even dogs seem to know that jealousy often makes life difficult for people. Attention and acknowledgment are vitally important to dogs. Dogs that have long been indulged and spoiled react overtly or covertly to diminished affection with pained withdrawal, with denial, or with aggressiveness, according to their temperament.

Solution: When a baby is on the way, the dog should not be squeezed out of the picture; even before the happy event, show it the baby's room and introduce it to the baby as early as the first day.

How Well Do You Know Your Dog?

Breed	Physical Exercise	Need to Keep Busy	Temperament	Suited to
Afghan Hound	a lot	medium	calm	experts
Airedale Terrier	a lot	a lot	active	experienced handlers
Beagle	medium	medium	active	beginners
Bernese Mountain Dog	medium	medium	calm	experienced handlers
Boxer	medium	a lot	active	experienced handlers
Chihuahua	little	little	medium	beginners
Chow Chow	little	little	calm	experts
Cocker Spaniel	medium	medium	active	beginners
Dachshund	medium	medium	medium	beginners
Dalmatian	a lot	medium	calm	experienced handlers
Doberman Pinscher	a lot	a lot	active	experts
Finnish Spitz	little	a lot	active	beginners
Fox Terrier	medium	a lot	active	experienced handlers
German Shepherd Dog	a lot	a lot	medium	experienced handlers
Golden Retriever	medium	medium	medium	beginners
Great Dane	medium	little	calm	experienced handlers
Kuvasz	medium	little	medium	experts
Labrador Retriever	medium	medium	medium	beginners
Newfoundland	little	little	calm	experienced handlers
Pekingese	little	little	medium	experienced handlers
Poodle	medium	a lot	active	beginners
Pug	little	medium	calm	beginners
Rottweiler	medium	medium	calm	experts
Saint Bernard	little	little	calm	experts
Schnauzer	medium	medium	medium	experienced handlers
Siberian Husky	a lot	medium	active	experts
West Highland White Terrier	little	medium	active	beginners
Yorkshire Terrier	little	little	active	beginners

Prescription to cure jealousy: Help dog and child trust each other, starting at an early age.

If the dog seems hesitant, don't force it to stay away, because that only aggravates feelings of jealousy; instead, in the presence of the child, pay attention to the dog, feed it, and pat it (at first on a leash, if necessary). Give the dog as much patting and attention as before and continue all the activities you do together.

A new life partner must earn the dog's trust step by step through feeding, walking, and brushing.

It's also helpful to pat the dog only in the presence of the new family member and otherwise pay no attention to it until it has connected positive attention to the supposed rival.

Rolling in Filth

Situation: You've just given the dog a bath, and at the first opportunity it rolls in the nearest cow manure.

Cause: Rolling in cow pies, manure, or carrion is instinctive. The dog hides its own scent that way as if with "perfume," which is the way its wild relatives can more easily hunt prey that has a sharp nose. Another logical reason is that dogs roll in dead animals in order to show the pack that they have found food.

Solution: As soon as possible, work with the leash-trained pup; look for a suitable spot or set out some raw fish or strong-smelling meat. At the first attempt to roll, pull forcefully on the leash and say "No!" At first, work with grown dogs only on a leash. Don't go near any filth without a leash until you've had several repetitions. Don't let determined rollers run free right after a bath; it's best to bathe them in the evening.

How to Handle Fighters

Situation: Excessive aggressiveness is more common among males than females.

Cause: Not enough contact with other dogs during puppyhood; overprotection by the owner (often including transferred anxiety); heightened competitiveness among male dogs.

Solution: When possible, let the dog off the leash, as the dog feels stronger linked to the owner by the leash. Don't run up to fighting dogs to separate them, or your excitement will be transferred to the dog. Instead, run 20 or 30 yards (18–27 m) away. Many dogs feel that they've been left in the lurch and they end the confrontation. Bring leashed dogs away from the stimulus; take them away or turn them aside so the dog can't stare at its antagonist (threatening posture). Then immediately command "Sit!" or "Lie down!" Get its attention in a soft voice and give it a treat. If necessary, throw water on fighting dogs or pull them up onto their hind legs. Don't step between them, and never hit the animals, since that only makes them fight harder.

Checklist
Help from the Professionals

Most problems with dogs cure themselves. "Home cures" are built on attention, understanding, sympathy, patience, and consistency, but help from behavior experts (veterinarian, breeder, dog psychologist, dog obedience school) is necessary in the following cases:

1 Bad behavior that has been tolerated for years. Owner's attempts to cure usually fail because the habits of dog and handler are deeply ingrained.

2 Severe problems in rank order: when dogs resist obedience training and become dangerous through heightened aggressiveness.

3 When first-time owners lack courage and practical experience, especially with large and self-assured dogs.

4 With self-destructive behavior: when dogs refuse food and affection (such as out of grief) or are completely fearful and shy (such as after a traumatic experience).

TIP

Sports and Dogs

Sports with dogs are the ideal fitness and health program for dog and owner. A requirement for participation is basic obedience training.

In most of these performance events, your dog must perform a series of exercises beginning with entry-level training and culminating in advanced competition with the possibility of awards and titles for your dog, and fun and bonding for you both. The sports can be strenuous, so get a clean bill of health from your doctor and your dog's veterinarian before you start.

Agility

Dog and handler together must negotiate a course with 12 to 20 obstacles such as tires, culverts, seesaws, tables, walls, and jumps. Purebred and mixed breed alike can participate on several levels.

Frisbee

This fast-moving sport involving both dog and owner can be enjoyed in the backyard, in the park, at the beach, or in regional and national competition.

Flyball

This is another exciting sport you can play with your dog one-on-one or in serious competition, in which the dog slaps the lever on a box of balls with its paw, the lever send a ball flying into the air, and the dog catches the ball and runs around a course with it.

Down with Boredom!

If dogs turn into regular vandals, nocturnal disturbers of the peace, persistent barkers, or high-strung wrecks, often there is just one cause—boredom. A dog with nothing to do will think of something, and that can get it into trouble. That's why the pack leader—the handler—should hand out assignments and tasks among the pack family, which is what the obedient dog expects from its master. A walk or five minutes of playing ball isn't enough. Competitive activity keeps body and mind in shape, offers the dog a chance to be useful to the owner, and provides the opportunity to earn titles and recognition.

How to Keep Various Breeds Properly Occupied

✔ Combination games: Dachshund, English Springer Spaniel, Fox Terrier, Miniature Pinscher, Schnauzer.

✔ Jogging, endurance training: All mid-sized breeds fond of running; for example, Airedale Terrier, Dalmatian, Labrador and Golden Retrievers, Siberian Husky.

✔ Obedience: All breeds, especially Border Collie and Golden Retriever.

✔ Guarding: Airedale Terrier, Boxer, Doberman Pinscher, German Shepherd Dog, Newfoundland, Rottweiler, and Saint Bernard.

✔ Guard duty: Bearded Collie, Bernese Mountain Dog, Doberman Pinscher, German Shepherd Dog.

Agility training promotes fitness in both you and your dog.

T I P

Hand Out the Assignments!

The puppy goes on discovery expeditions and develops its own activities, and that's an important part of its development. The grown dog generally does nothing on its own initiative. According to its pack mentality, it's up to the pack leader to determine what has to be done and who does which job. That's why it's always the owner's duty to set up the activity schedule. Your dog's willingness to adapt gives you the security of knowing it will gladly accept practically every task you give it.

Variety Is Good for Dogs

A stroll through the city, a vacation trip with the family, meeting dogs at a playground, frequent house guests—above all, these are new situations that demand attentiveness, adaptability, tolerance, self-confidence, and readiness to cooperate. A day in the city is more exciting and demanding (in a positive way) than a five-mile run next to a bicycle. Dogs that regularly have to use their wits, as with competitive activities (see page 52), are happier and more stable than those that are allowed merely to run free and aimlessly.

Neglected Dogs

Situation: Some dogs scarcely notice their surroundings, while others ignore all commands, are rebellious, or refuse to obey.

Cause: Dogs that feel neglected become withdrawn. Typical defiance and defense reactions include indifference, resistance to commands, and destructiveness.

Solution: Severity will not help. Try to break down the dog's resistance through appealing invitations to do things together. Perhaps an obedience course will work if the dog realizes that it once again fits in.

The best prescription for refreshing the relationship is play. Playing is as natural to a dog as sleeping and eating. It strengthens its trust and helps it work off pent-up aggression; also the dog feels challenged and accepted (see pages 58–59). Even if there are external reasons for neglecting your dog, such as a lack of free time, draw up a weekly schedule and check it to see where your dog could accompany you. You'll be amazed at how much you can do together.

Persistent Barkers

Situation: Dogs that bark continuously annoy owner and neighbors.

Cause: Barking can be an inherited talent (as with many terriers and spitz breeds), but

The desire to retrieve is in every Labrador Retriever's blood.

A Schedule for Keeping Busy

Possible Activities ★ = recommended ○ = less suitable	In the House	In the Yard	On a Walk	At Play	Training Facility
Hide and seek (objects)	★	★	★	○	★
Hide and seek (people)	★	★	★	○	★
Combination games	★	★	★	○	○
Tracking (scent trails)	○	★	★	○	○
Fetch	★	★	★	○	★
Pulling sleds or wagons	○	○	★	○	○
Guarding items	★	★	○	○	★
Carrying stick, bag, etc.	○	○	★	○	○
Agility	○	★	○	○	★
Balance test	○	★	★	○	★
Playing ball with human	★	★	★	○	★
Active games (such as Frisbee)	○	★	★	★	★
Refresher training course	★	★	★	★	★
Fitness run	○	○	★	○	○
Running beside bicycle	○	○	★	○	○
Free play with other dogs	○	○	★	★	★
Puppy training	○	○	○	○	★
Swimming	○	○	★	○	○

constant barking can be the result of faulty training. For example, if sounding off is encouraged by praise in certain situations, the dog doesn't connect the praise to the situation, but rather to the barking. Often, dogs also bark out of boredom, and the more they bark, the more they like doing it. Sometimes, desirable alarm barking becomes self-sustaining and dogs bark for no good reason. Usually the tendency to bark increases with age.

Solution: Dogs that bark when they're left alone for a long time need something to do; therefore, teach your dog the commands "Down!" and "Stay!" and give it an object such as a sweater or handbag to watch over. Learning to be alone is an important lesson in basic training (see Fear of Being Left Alone, page

33). Many dogs bark to get attention. Even if you get angry at them, they take it as success. Yelling at overexcited barkers also has a negative effect; the person's excitement stimulates the dog even more. Spraying water, or setting up a screen between the yard and the street, usually helps only for a short time. Instead, reward the dog every time it stops barking. When it barks, give the command "Down!" Dogs feel less self-assured when they are lying down and don't want to draw extra attention to themselves. Offer them chew toys or food. A full mouth cuts down on "talkativeness," and a full belly makes a dog sleepy. If excessive barking is rooted in problems during puppyhood, the dog needs as much contact as possible at play and taking walks with other dogs. In dog obedience school a dog learns how to integrate into a pack. Barkers are not accepted by the community and are annoying to everyone.

A War of Nerves over Food

Situation: Even though they are provided with the best, many dogs refuse to eat their food.

Cause: Dogs prefer food they know and trust. So you should always give them the same food. Refusal to eat is usually connected to a desire to share the people's meals.

Solution: Even young dogs have to learn that there are established times for feeding—at first, four servings a day, and later one or two. Dogs should always be fed in the same place and where they won't be disturbed.

Since eating is a communicative event for a dog, it may be allowed to sit near the

Dogs that refuse to eat require lots of firmness and persistence on the part of the handler.

kitchen table, but without begging and without ever getting any morsels from the table. If your dog likes a particular type of food, don't change it unless it is necessary (for example, in case of sickness, diet, or incompatibility). Be tough if your dog refuses its food just because it takes a fancy to your steak.

Important: Refusal to eat can be a symptom of illness. Take the dog to the veterinarian if it leaves its food untouched for more than 48 hours.

Destructiveness

Situation: The dog scratches doors, shreds pillows, gnaws chair legs. Some dogs have a stubborn urge to reduce your house to splinters.

Cause: A training program for puppies addresses the tendency to chew (see page 38). Later, a young dog tries to soothe teething discomfort by chewing. With grown dogs,

destructiveness may be caused by fear of separation. Often, dogs start gnawing out of boredom, and after a while chewing becomes a regular part of their behavior.

Solution: Tired dogs don't get into trouble! Before a dog is left alone, it should burn up some energy on a walk or in sports and games. Put the dog into a small space to provide as few outside stimuli as possible, such as other dogs seen through the window and noises from the entryway and stairs. With puppies, also provide distraction and substitution with hard rubber chew toys. With grown dogs, give chew toys and spray or wipe forbidden places with lemon, bitter substances, or perfume. If you catch the dog red-handed, a shot from a water pistol helps.

Fright Therapy: Loosely wedge under the table top an old table leg or a branch, to which you have tied some empty tin cans. When the dog bites it, the cans fall with a crash. You should leave the room beforehand so that the dog doesn't associate the action with you.

Attacking chair legs or rugs is a so-called crossover behavior that's triggered by fear of being left alone. In this case, first deal with the fear of separation (see Fear of Being Left Alone, page 33).

Banish Boredom with Play

A dog of medium size, such as a German Shepherd Dog, needs at least two (and preferably three) hours of activity; otherwise, it looks for alternatives such as digging in the yard, gnawing furniture, continuous begging, and peskiness, or it becomes rebellious and disobedient. It can have its activ-

To build the dog's confidence, always praise it when it accomplishes a task.

ity deficit reduced by playing. Specific multiple tasks capture all of its attention.

✔ Find and fetch: Hide a ball or favorite toy in the house, such as in a box, behind a cupboard, or under the rug.

✔ Multiple tasks: Pull an object on a cord several times through a large pipe, then leave it in the middle of the pipe and have the dog find it.

Another possibility: Roll a ball under a barrier so that the dog has to make a detour to get it back.

Always reward cooperation, even if the dog is not successful.

Note: Excessive play can heighten a dog's need for activity, and therefore work contrary to your aims.

A dog gets rid of surplus energy in the car because it's bored.

Driving School for Hyperactive Dogs

Before going for a ride, give barkers and hyperactive dogs a chance to use up some energy in sport and play.

Dogs that haven't had a chance to let off steam, or that view the car as their private property, often bark at the slightest provocation. Many become frantic if strange people or other dogs come close to the car, and often scratch or shred seats and clothing. If you have such a demon, take it for a training drive on back roads. Stop at every disturbance or attempt at barking. At the same time, a second person should reprimand the dog with a "neck bite" (see page 15) or squirt it with a water pistol. Do not continue to drive until the dog is completely calm. When it remains calm, praise it and give it treats. It's best to put the dog in a travel crate with hard sides for long rides in the car.

Training a Dog to Be a Good Eater

When dogs reject their food, it may be because they need more affection.

Most dogs that are fussy eaters are too fat. They are used to having their feeding bowl always filled and taking only the best from it, and on top of that, they always get treats whether or not they have earned them.

Give your dog a measured amount of food in its dish. If it ceases to eat—short pauses are permissible—take the bowl away. Give the dog nothing more until the next meal. If there are leftovers, give the dog less at the next feeding. If it eagerly licks the bowl clean, give it a little more next time.

Walking on a seesaw is an exercise that requires a dog's full attention.

acquaintances among people and animals. Mini-exercises for daily walks include balancing on tree trunks, hiding games, and slalom-run around trees.

Tip: Set up an agility course in the yard (seesaw, jump, tunnel, hurdles, dog walk).

Important: Establish definite playtimes. Afterwards, put away all toys. End each play session with "Sit!" for about three minutes, plus patting and praise. That way the dog learns when it can let off steam.

A Day Job for Night Workers

Dogs that don't sleep at night often don't feel like going to bed. They need a day job. A healthy dog of normal weight does not get worn out at play or even on a long walk. Activities that require its entire attention are more demanding: a regular basic training refresher, development programs at dog training facilities, scent tracking, searches, guard duty, visiting unfamiliar places, making new

Only the handler determines when it's time for play.

*This puppy is helping itself.
A well-aimed squirt from a water
pistol will stop this thievery.*

Useful Addresses*

American Kennel Club
5580 Centerview Drive, Suite 200
Raleigh, NC 27606-3390
919-233-9780

The Canadian Kennel Club
100-89 Skyway Avenue
Etobicoke, Ontario M9W6R4
Canada
416-675-5511

American Field
542 South Dearborn Street
Chicago, IL 60605
312-663-9797

United Kennel Club
100 East Kilgore Road
Kalamazoo, MI 49002-5584
616-343-9020

National Bird Dog Museum
505 West Highway 57
P.O. Box 744
Grand Junction, TN 88039
901-764-2058

American Rare Breeds Association
9921 Frank Tippett Road
Cheltenham, MD 20623
301-868-5718

*Addresses of breed clubs and
other dog-related organizations
are available from the associations
mentioned above.

Periodicals

AKC Gazette
Subscriptions: 919-233-9767

Dog Fancy
P.O. Box 53264
Boulder, CO 80322-3264

Dog World
29 North Wacker Drive
Chicago, IL 60606

Off-Lead
204 Lewis Street
Canastota, NY 13032
800-241-7619

Books

American Kennel Club. *The Complete Dog Book.* New York, New York: Howell Book House, 1992.

Ammen, Amy. *Training in No Time: An Expert's Approach to Effective Dog Training for Hectic Life Styles.* New York, New York: Howell Book House, 1995.

Bailey, Gwen. *The Well Behaved Dog.* Hauppauge, New York: Barron's Educational Series, 1998.

Davis, Kathy Diamond. *Responsible Dog Ownership.* New York, New York: Howell Book House, 1994.

Smith, Cheryl S. *Pudgy Pooch, Picky Pooch.* Hauppauge, New York: Barron's Educational Series, Inc., 1998.

Taunton, Stephanie J. and Cheryl S. Smith. *The Trick Is in the Training.* Hauppauge, New York: Barron's Educational Series, Inc., 1998.

Author

Zoologist and journalist Dr. Gerd Ludwig is editor of *Animal* magazine.

Photographer

The photos in this book are by Monika Wegler, a renowned photographer, journalist, and author of animal books. In recent years, her work has included animal portraits and studies on behavior and movement of cats and dogs.

Artist

Renate Holzner works as a freelance illustrator in Germany. Her broad repertory goes from line drawing to photographically realistic illustrations and computer graphics.

Photos: Book Cover and Contents

Page 1: Girl with seven-week-old puppy. Pages 2–3: Family with two-and-a-half-year-old Saint Bernard. Pages 4–5: Bearded Collie jumping over agility hurdle. Page 64: Girl playing with five-month-old Golden Retriever.

Cover Photo: Barbara Augello

English translation © Copyright 1998 by Barron's Educational Series, Inc.

Original title of the book in German is
Mein Hund macht was er will
Copyright © 1997 by Gräfe und Unzer Verlag GmbH, Munich

All inquiries should be addressed to:
Barron's Educational Series, Inc.
250 Wireless Boulevard
Hauppauge, New York 11788

http://www.barronseduc.com

Important Note
Is Your Dog Healthy?

Changes in behavior can be the result of sickness, physical impairment, or pain. Nighttime restlessness is frequently caused by heart and circulatory infirmities; sudden aggressiveness can be triggered by pain; loss of control suggests problems with stomach, intestines, or kidneys. Also, behavior irregularities can lead to illness, especially when they last for some time, as with listlessness and refusal to eat. Every dog that displays noticeable changes in behavior, such as suddenly giving up usual habits, should be seen by the veterinarian. Corrective handling as described in this book should be undertaken only after the veterinarian has determined that the dog is free of illness or injury.

Library of Congress Catalog Card No. 98-4267

International Standard Book Number 0-7641-0663-5

Library of Congress Cataloging-in-Publication Data
Ludwig, Gerd.
    [Mein Hund Macht Was Er Will. English]
    Sit! Stay! / Gerd Ludwig ; translated from the German by Eric A. Bye.
        p.   cm. — (A complete pet owner's manual)
    Includes index.
    ISBN 0-7641-0663-5
    1. Dogs—Behavior. 2. Dogs—Training. I. Title. II. Series.
    636.7'088'7—dc21   98-4267
                                    CIP

Printed in Hong Kong

9 8 7 6 5

1 Male of female dog: Which one is the best partner for me?

Males are more confident and strong-willed; females are gentler and more companionable. Both, however, require consistent training.

2 My dog is disobedient. What am I doing wrong?

Dogs, as pack animals, demand leadership qualities in their boss (balanced nature, love, consistency). If a person appears indulgent and indecisive, the dog will take over the leadership role.

3 I'm the only one our dog will obey; it couldn't care less about the rest of the family. Will it ever become a good family dog?

Very few breeds fixate on a single master. Affection, care, feeding, play, and sport can create the necessary bonding.

4 What can be done about a dog that fights?

The best thing for fighters is to learn socialization in large groups of dogs, as in dog obedience classes. The handler should stay out of the vicinity, because his or her presence will support the dog's feelings of toughness.

5 Is there hope for stubborn wanderers?

Dogs that roam usually lack a strong tie to a specific person. They need variety, occupation, and stimulation. Exceptions are females in heat and lovesick males.